The
Reagans

by
Cass R. Sandak

CRESTWOOD HOUSE
New York

Maxwell Macmillan Canada
Toronto

Maxwell Macmillan International
New York Oxford Singapore Sydney

Library of Congress Cataloging-in-Publication Data
Sandak, Cass R.
  The Reagans / by Cass R. Sandak. — 1st ed.
    p. cm. — (First families)
  Includes bibliographical references and index.
  Summary: An account of the private life and political career of Ronald Reagan, with information on his family relationships, particularly with his second wife, Nancy Davis Reagan.
  ISBN 0-89686-646-7
  1. Reagan, Ronald, 1911–   —Juvenile literature. 2. Reagan family—Juvenile literature. 3. Presidents—United States—Biography—Juvenile literature. 4. United States—Politics and government—1981–1989—Juvenile literature. [1. Reagan, Ronald, 1911–   . 2. Reagan, Nancy, 1923–   . 3. Presidents. 4. First ladies.] I. Title.
II. Series: Sandak, Cass R.   First families.
E877.S255   1993
973.927'092—dc20
[B]   92-37838

Photo Credits
Cover: AP—Wide World Photos
AP—Wide World Photos: 4, 7, 10, 11, 13, 14, 16, 18, 20, 22, 24, 26, 30, 31, 36, 39, 45
The Bettmann Archive: 27, 34, 41

Macmillan Publishing Company
866 Third Avenue
New York, NY 10022

Maxwell Macmillan Canada, Inc.
1200 Eglinton Avenue East
Suite 200
Don Mills, Ontario M3C 3N1

CRESTWOOD HOUSE

Macmillan Publishing Company is part of the Maxwell Communication Group of Companies.

Produced by Flying Fish Studio

Printed in the United States of America

First edition

10 9 8 7 6 5 4 3 2 1

Contents

A Secret Service agent raises his automatic weapon during the attempted assassination of President Reagan.

A Close Call

President Ronald Reagan had been in office only 70 days when an attempt was made on his life. A young man named John Hinckley fired six shots as Reagan was leaving a Washington hotel. Reagan was injured, but not seriously. His press secretary, James Brady, was also shot. He, however, was not so lucky. As a result of the shooting, Brady was permanently disabled.

The assassination attempt took place at 2:30 P.M. outside the Washington Hilton. Reagan had just spoken to a luncheon meeting of union leaders. There was a moment of panic as shots rang out, smoke filled the air and people screamed and ducked for cover.

A bullet penetrated the president's chest. It struck a rib and passed into his lower left lung, just inches from his heart. Fortunately a limousine was waiting. Secret Service agents shoved the president into the car and then sped off to George Washington University Hospital. The president was able to walk into the emergency room. Then he collapsed before nurses and doctors could lift him onto a stretcher.

Reagan's wife, Nancy, reached the hospital by three o'clock, having had a premonition that something was wrong. She arrived distraught, but she gave surgeons permission to operate. The surgery lasted two hours. Twelve days after the operation, the president was released from the hospital.

As a result of the attempted assassination, security around the president was tightened. Reagan's popularity —already high—went up several notches.

It probably took some acting on the part of the president to convince an anxious world that he was fine. But that part was easy. For the first time in history the president of the United States was a former movie star.

"Dutch" Reagan

Ronald Wilson Reagan was born on February 6, 1911, in Tampico, Illinois, in a five-room apartment above a store. His brother, John Neil (known as Neil), was two years older.

The father of the future president was John "Jack" Edward Reagan. He was a Roman Catholic and a Democrat, both rare in the small midwestern towns where the Reagans lived when Ronald was growing up. He was hardworking but unreliable. Jack Reagan was an alcoholic. When he could get work it was usually as a shoe salesman. He had his own store for a while, until he went bankrupt during the depression. For some years in the 1930s Mr. Reagan worked for the Works Progress Administration (WPA), a government agency.

Reagan's mother was Nelle Wilson, and her background was Scots-Irish Presbyterian. She was devout and spent a

*John Reagan,
sons Neil and
Ronald, and
his wife, Nelle*

great deal of time doing charity work. Mrs. Reagan saw that the boys attended plays and lectures. She kept the family together through the force of her optimistic and cheerful personality.

Neil was raised a Catholic, even though the boy's father had stopped going to church. Mrs. Reagan raised young Ronald as a Protestant, like herself.

Jack Reagan gave his younger boy the name Dutch. This was because the round-faced infant looked to him like "a fat little Dutchman." The name stuck with Reagan for most of his teenage years and even into college. In fact, it wasn't until he went to Hollywood that the name was completely dropped.

One of Ronald Reagan's most painful early memories was from when he was 11 years old. He found his father drunk and unconscious on the front porch. Reagan dragged his father into the house. The event left a lasting impression. From an early age Ronald Reagan understood the problems that alcohol could cause.

The Reagans lived a very modest life. As long as Jack held a job, the family was able to eat. When Ronald was only nine, the family moved to Dixon, Illinois, just 100 miles from Chicago. From that time forward, Reagan always referred to Dixon as his hometown. In Dixon he completed elementary school and then went on to high school, where he was elected president of his senior class.

As a child Ronald was very nearsighted, although the family didn't realize it until he was 12. When young Ronald began to wear glasses, many of his problems were solved as the world came into focus.

Reagan was a bright child and a quick study. He had an almost photographic memory. This helped him in reading, dramatics and schoolwork. He learned to swim at the Dixon YMCA and soon became a skilled lifeguard. Reagan worked as a lifeguard for seven summers during and after high school. He saved a total of 77 people from drowning and became something of a local hero.

Sports mattered to Reagan a great deal. He was not an outstanding athlete, but coaches and fellow team members were impressed with his determination and spirit. However, his poor eyesight kept him from becoming a sports star.

As a youngster Reagan also liked going to movies on Saturday afternoons. Films were still silent, and it cost an adult 25 cents to see a movie, while a youngster could get in for a dime.

Eureka

Reagan's first love was a girl named Margaret "Mugs" Cleaver. She was a schoolmate and daughter of a local Dixon minister. The two planned to attend the same college together. Eureka College represented a bright dream of a better life to Reagan. He had visited the campus along with Mugs and had been impressed by the stately and serene academic atmosphere. They spent two years together at Eureka. But, on a summer vacation trip traveling in Europe, Mugs met and married an attorney.

Reagan's hopes were dashed, but he finished college as his brother and mother had both encouraged him to do. At Eureka he majored in social science and economics.

Reagan persuaded Neil to get a college education as well. Neil finally gave in and joined Ron at Eureka, where his younger brother showed him the ropes. There was probably some resentment on Neil's part that Ron was taking the lead, but the two remained close. Neil later became a vice president of a giant international advertising agency, McCann Erickson.

To his credit, Reagan worked his way through college. He had a sports scholarship, which paid half his tuition. He made up the other half by working in the kitchen of his fraternity house. Unfortunately his grades suffered because of all the time he devoted to work and sports.

Some of Reagan's happiest times were spent at Eureka. In later years Reagan often returned to the college for visits. He also gave the school strong financial support.

Reagan graduated from college in 1932. By this time,

Hundreds of men wait in a long line for some soup and bread. Many people lost their jobs during the Great Depression, including Ronald Reagan's father.

America had plunged into the Great Depression. During the depression Reagan's father lost his job. For a time the Reagans lived in one room and Mrs. Reagan cooked on a hot plate. That was Ronald Reagan's first taste of poverty. The family's Sunday dinners consisted of pieces of meat discarded by the butcher. A soup bone would provide meals to last the family for a whole week.

After College

Reagan's first job after college was as a radio announcer. He hitchhiked to Chicago looking for announcing jobs, but was told to gain experience in a smaller place. He then went to Davenport, Iowa, where he began his radio career. As a sportscaster he was a commentator on more than 600 baseball games. He even reported on games he didn't watch, with made-up descriptions of the players and events. But his audiences loved listening to him.

Radio broadcaster Ronald Reagan at the microphone

Just as soon as he had an income, Reagan helped his parents and his brother by sending money to them. During this time Reagan took up horseback riding. Reagan joined a U. S. Army special cavalry unit. He practiced his riding for two years before taking a test to qualify. It was one instance that showed Reagan's determination. Later on, this skilled horsemanship helped him land roles in Western films.

In 1937 Reagan was reporting on the Chicago Cubs' spring training camp on Catalina Island off the coast of southern California. With a friend's help he approached a Hollywood studio for a screen test. The test won him a contract with Warner Brothers.

The Movie Star

Just a short time later Reagan appeared in his first movie. It was the first of 53 feature films in which Reagan would appear. The industry responded to his rugged good looks, self-effacing manner and trained speaking voice. In his first year in Hollywood Reagan made eight movies.

For the first time he found that he had more than enough money. Reagan felt so confident of his future in movies that he quickly asked his parents to join him in California so they could enjoy the warm climate there.

Even in films that were not very good, Reagan often won praise for his performances. Within a few years he had made some major films. *Brother Rat, King's Row* and *Knute Rockne—All American* were among the best. In *Knute Rockne* Reagan played the character of a legendary Notre Dame

Ronald Reagan as football player George Gipp in Knute Rockne—All American

football player named George Gipp, known as the Gipper. A famous line in the film said, "Win one for the Gipper." Reagan would later use this inspirational slogan while he was campaigning for political office.

Ronald Reagan and wife-to-be Jane Wyman apply for their marriage license.

The First Mrs. Reagan

In 1938, while they were both acting in minor roles in the movie *Brother Rat*, Ronald Reagan met Jane Wyman. Slightly younger than Ronald, Miss Wyman came from Independence, Missouri. Jane Wyman had been born Sarah Jane Fulks in 1914. She came to Hollywood, changed her name and was given a lot of studio publicity. Like so many pretty women in the 1930s, she was sure she could become a big movie star. She was, in fact, beginning a major career as an actress. She had had a brief first marriage that was over by the time she met Ronald Reagan.

14

Reagan's marriage to Jane Wyman took place on January 26, 1940. They were wed at Forest Lawn in Glendale, California, in a chapel patterned after a Scottish country church. The reception was held at the home of gossip columnist Louella Parsons.

The next year, 1941, marked a high point in Reagan's film career. He received more fan mail than James Cagney, the very popular actor. With Reagan's prodding, the studio gave his father a job answering his son's fan mail. Sacks of it came to the studio each week.

In 1942, during World War II, Reagan was called to active duty in the U.S. Army. He served as a captain. Because of his bad eyesight the army found him unsuitable for combat. They decided that Reagan could be more useful making war films. Accordingly he was assigned to nearby Burbank, a center of movie studios. This meant that Reagan could commute home nightly to his family. In Burbank Reagan narrated Army Air Corps training films.

The Reagans' daughter was born on January 4, 1941. She was named Maureen. In March of 1945 the couple adopted a son, Michael. Reagan's first ranch was a modest eight acres near Van Nuys, California, not far from Hollywood. It was the first of three he has owned. Reagan found ranching a wholesome change from the glitter and uncertainty of Hollywood.

In the late 1940s Reagan began to take an interest in organizations set up to benefit screen actors. He became politically active. It was the time of the "Red Scare" in Hollywood. Many people thought the film industry was

Ronald Reagan, president of the Screen Actors Guild, waiting to testify in Washington during the "Red Scare," when certain politicians thought Hollywood was full of communists

full of communists. Reagan testified in Washington on behalf of people from the entertainment world who were not communists.

Reagan became president of the Screen Actors Guild in 1947. The guild is actually a labor union. Thus far, Reagan is the only president to come to the White House with labor union experience.

In the same year he nearly died from a bout of viral pneumonia. Only the efforts of a heroic nurse pulled him through.

About this time Jane Wyman's career began to move faster than Reagan's. Hers stood to become an even bigger

Hollywood name, causing some strain on their marriage. Miss Wyman also felt her husband was spending too much time on his work. One of Hollywood's golden couples divorced in 1948. When the Reagans split, Miss Wyman gained custody of both children. In the same year as the divorce, Miss Wyman won an Oscar for best actress, in the film *Johnny Belinda*.

The Second Mrs. Reagan

Both the divorce and his flagging film career caused Reagan some pain. He remained one of Hollywood's eligible bachelors, but only for a short time.

Ronald Reagan met an actress named Nancy Davis when she approached him for help. Reagan was then active in the Screen Actors Guild. Miss Davis was concerned because her name had been repeatedly linked with Hollywood organizations thought to be friendly toward communism. It turned out there was another actress with the same name!

Nancy was small and slender, with dark hair and wide hazel eyes. When Reagan and Nancy had their first date, he was on crutches from injuries he suffered in a charity baseball game. Reagan's second wedding took place on March 4, 1952, when he married Nancy Davis.

Nancy had been born Anne Frances Robbins on July 6, 1921, in New York City. Nancy herself claims she was born in 1923, but evidence (her birth certificate) strongly suggests

Ronald and Nancy Reagan on their wedding day

the earlier date. Nancy's father, Kenneth Robbins, was a car salesman. Nancy's mother, Edith Luckett, was an actress. But her parents' marriage was not a happy one and ended in divorce while Nancy was still a baby.

For the first eight years of her life, Nancy was raised by an aunt. During this time her mother was often on tour acting in plays.

Nancy was only eight in 1929 when her mother married Dr. Loyal Davis, a prominent Chicago neurosurgeon. Nancy was a flower girl at the wedding. By this time Nancy's mother had given up her stage career. When Nancy was 14 her stepfather legally adopted her. Nancy remained very close to Dr. Davis. He was a great influence on her life until his death during her years in the White House.

After her graduation from prestigious Smith College in Massachusetts, Nancy began an acting career. She appeared in several plays in New York in the 1940s before going to Hollywood to seek a career in films. Her first movie, in 1949, was called *The Doctor and the Girl*.

Less than eight months after their wedding, Ronald and Nancy Reagan had their first child. Born on October 22, 1952, and christened Patricia Ann Davis Reagan, she came to be known as Patti Davis. Their second child, Ronald Prescott Reagan, was born nearly six years later, on May 28, 1958. After this, Nancy gave up acting to become a full-time wife and mother. Her film career, though promising, never really developed in a significant way.

The End of the Movies

In the early 1950s Reagan's movie career began to taper off. Television became a competitor for movies, and the old film studios lost much of their power and luster. Perhaps because Reagan was a union leader, studio heads were reluctant to employ him, fearing he might turn out to be a troublemaker.

Reagan as a singing waiter during his brief stint in a Las Vegas nightclub act

Reagan went through a difficult period when no movie roles came in. He tried working for a few months in Las Vegas nightclub acts, but he couldn't sing, dance or tell jokes, so he served as emcee for a slapstick comedy act. With his radio announcer's voice he was a natural for this role. Although the work was lucrative, it was humiliating and Reagan soon gave it up.

By 1954 Reagan had switched from the large screen to the small screen. He became the spokesperson for General Electric Theater, a half-hour weekly television show. In his role as host he would introduce each show and occasionally act in one. Nancy sometimes appeared in the dramas and did commercials. A blend of drama and comedy, the highly successful and popular show paid Reagan $125,000 a year.

Reagan was under contract to General Electric for eight years. Not only did he host the program, but he spent much of his time making speeches on behalf of the company, one of the world's largest. After all, he was a well-known actor and was completely at ease in front of audiences.

Entrance into Politics

Reagan's father had been a Democrat, and President Franklin D. Roosevelt was one of young Ronald's heroes. As late as 1950 Reagan was still a member of the Democratic party. For most of this time Reagan was also a liberal. But sometime in the late 1950s he began to shift more and more to the conservative side of politics. By 1962 he had become a registered Republican.

Reagan's formal entrance into politics was marked by his speech in support of Republican presidential candidate Barry Goldwater during the 1964 campaign. During the speech Reagan was relaxed and confident. His single appearance raised $1 million and garnered a lot of publicity. His address impressed many observers. Among these was Robert Altschuler, a powerful figure in California politics. He was the first to see Reagan's potential as a politician. As a result Reagan was tapped in 1966 to run for governor of California.

California Governor

The newcomer to politics announced in January of 1966 that he would run as a candidate for governor of California. He won the primary election with great ease, ensuring that his name would appear on the ballot. He went on to defeat Governor Pat Brown, 3.7 million votes to 2.7 million. It was a stunning victory.

With little effort Reagan became governor of one of the nation's most influential and rapidly growing states. He,

Reagan shows the victory sign upon learning that he won his bid for governor of California.

Nancy and the children moved to Sacramento. There, however, they found the governor's mansion so uncomfortable that they rented their own house in a different part of the city.

It was during this time that Reagan placed a jar of jelly beans in his office. Guests were encouraged to dip into the jar. The jelly bean tradition followed Reagan to the White House a few years later.

In two terms as California governor, Reagan successfully reformed the tax and welfare apparatus of the country's most populous state. He was able to revamp California's vast and complex education system. He also turned the state's budget around. From operating at a deficit, the state's treasury grew to show a $550 million surplus.

Reagan ran for a second term and won just as easily as the first time. But he decided he would not run for the office a third time. So in January 1975 he left the governor's office after serving two terms. He and his advisers had something bigger in mind.

The Reagans moved to a new ranch, south of Los Angeles in Riverside County. It covered almost 700 acres. They divided time between the ranch and their lovely home on the coast in Pacific Palisades. As Nancy did not really like horses or horseback riding, she preferred the Palisades house. Reagan often went on speaking engagements. He also wrote a weekly newspaper column.

Wanting to Be President

Even while he was governor, Reagan was eager to run as a Republican candidate for president. But Richard Nixon was a popular president and Reagan had no alternative but to wait his turn.

In 1973 Nixon had to replace his vice president, Spiro Agnew. Nixon chose Gerald Ford. Public opinion then forced Nixon to resign from the presidency in 1974. Ford succeeded him. As the 1976 election approached, Reagan decided to campaign against Ford for the Republican nomination, but lost his bid. Ford was then defeated in the general election by the Democratic candidate, Jimmy Carter.

As the 1980 election drew nearer, Reagan decided he would again campaign, and he vowed that this time he would win. Although Reagan was a good speaker, his campaign did not begin well. No one took him seriously.

And he did not seem to be aware of the public's needs. As a result, no one cared what he was doing. He quickly recognized his problems, and did an about-face. He vigorously threw himself into the campaign, and suddenly everyone sat up and took notice.

Reagan had little trouble winning the race against Carter. President Carter's term had been troubled by inflation and a failing economy. The United States had lost face in the world when Iran took American hostages at the embassy in Teheran. United States prestige suffered even more after an abortive attempt to free the hostages.

President Carter seemed weak and projected an image of American weakness. Reagan began talking tough—about tax cuts and military buildups. Even before he was elected, his economic program was referred to as "Reaganomics." Reagan's ideas included deregulation and encouragement of industry, or supply-side economics. Just two weeks before the election, a debate between Reagan and Carter showed Reagan in his best form.

So it was not much of a surprise in November 1980 when Reagan trounced Carter. The popular vote was 44 million to 35 million. The electoral college victory was even stronger: 489 to 49 votes.

Reagan was the oldest president ever to be elected to office. He still rode horses and exercised daily. He had a thick head of reddish brown hair that he denied was ever dyed. Most people thought he looked much younger than his 69 years.

Ronald Reagan campaigned vigorously during the 1980 presidential campaign.

Ronald Reagan is sworn in as president as Nancy looks on.

Hollywood on the Potomac

Ronald Reagan was inaugurated on January 20, 1981. Reagan's inaugural speech underscored the theme of American renewal. The new president said, "We are not, as some would have us believe, doomed to an inevitable decline."

Almost immediately a change took place in the White House. An atmosphere of elegance and glamour returned. Where entertaining under the Carters had been informal and relaxed, under the Reagans old-time formality came back.

The Reagans entertained on a grand scale. Their dinners blended Washington society and the Hollywood elite. They always had special menus prepared. Nancy would often test the menu for a large dinner on her unsuspecting husband.

Reagan usually rose at about 8:00 A.M., and he and Nancy enjoyed breakfast together in their living quarters. He then went to the Oval Office, where his top advisers were usually waiting. Reagan did not like details, so he was more dependent than many presidents on his advisers. He held a briefing at 9:45 A.M. This might be followed by a Cabinet meeting in a nearby room. There were many times, it has been reported, when Reagan nodded off during these meetings. A simple lunch was followed by an afternoon of meetings and discussions.

Never a workaholic, Reagan was lucky in his advisers. General counsel Edwin Meese, White House chief of staff James Baker and deputy chief of staff Michael Deaver were all strong people who guided the president.

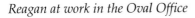
Reagan at work in the Oval Office

Reagan had a forceful vice president in George Bush and relied heavily on him. Bush had more control over U.S. foreign policy than any previous vice president.

From the beginning, Nancy Reagan played an active role in her husband's affairs. She insisted on knowing his schedule and often demanded political information from his advisers.

After a busy week the Reagans often boarded a helicopter on the White House lawn on Friday afternoon. The chopper would take them to Camp David in Maryland. The presidential retreat was about 30 minutes away.

The Reagan Years

In 1981 Reagan engineered a major tax cut. It was felt this would stimulate the economy. But soon the country was in a major recession. So Reagan turned around in 1982 and ordered a tax increase! This seemed to work, and by 1983 the nation began an economic recovery. The country experienced boom times, at least in some sectors of the economy.

At the beginning of Reagan's term, relations between the United States and the Soviet Union were poor. To counter what Reagan felt was the ever-present threat from Soviet missiles, he proposed a plan. It was officially called SDI, or Strategic Defense Initiative. It was popularly known as Star Wars. SDI was a complex network of weapon interception devices meant to make war obsolete.

Then in 1985 Mikhail Gorbachev became a major player in Soviet politics. Soon a period known as *glasnost*, or openness, began. Summit meetings were held between the two nations in 1985 and 1986 to help bring about accord. During much of this time and after, both powers tried earnestly to keep world peace.

Nicaragua was a trouble spot early in Reagan's presidency. The administration gave secret aid to the Contras, a group fighting the communist-led Sandinista government. As it had done in Vietnam, the United States was once again stepping in to fight communism. But many Americans were suspicious that American soldiers would have to die in a hopeless cause. The scars of Vietnam had not completely healed.

Leftists again provoked American intervention in a little-known outpost. The tiny Caribbean island of Grenada was threatened with a coup that might endanger the lives of Americans there. The insurgents, however, were easily overcome. In a few short months peace had been restored.

Terrorism grew to frightening proportions during the Reagan years. More and more Americans were taken hostage at strategic places around the world. Almost 250 Americans were killed in Beirut, Lebanon, in 1983 when terrorists drove trucks loaded with explosives into the U.S. Marine headquarters there. Fifty more servicemen were killed at a French compound nearby. In 1985 the Palestine Liberation Organization (PLO) hijacked a cruise ship, the *Achille Lauro*, and killed an American tourist. The event aroused outrage, particularly in the United States.

U.S. marines carry the body of a fellow soldier out of the rubble, after terrorist explosives destroyed a building in Beirut. Almost 250 Americans on a peacekeeping mission died in the attack.

In April 1986 Reagan made a bold move when U.S. warplanes were sent to put an end to terrorism by bombing Libya. It was a strike against Muammar Qaddafi in retaliation for the Libyan dictator's program of state-sponsored terrorism.

Then in December 1988 Pan Am flight 103 was blown out of the sky over Lockerbie, Scotland. All told, 300 people were killed both on the plane and on the ground. Many of these acts were committed by radical political groups.

Reagan's position on terrorist activity was publicly strong: There would be no negotiation. With that came a pledge to punish international terrorists quickly.

Libyans carry coffins containing the bodies of adults and children killed in the bombing of Libya by U.S. planes.

Back in late 1986 a scandal was uncovered that threatened the president's credibility. About two years earlier the Reagan administration had agreed to sell arms to Iran if that country would release American hostages. Much of the profit from the sale of weapons was diverted to help the Contras fighting in Nicaragua. Thus the episode became known as the Iran-Contra affair.

The whole event threatened to bring President Reagan severe censure. The Tower Commission was set up to investigate the affair. Much of the blame, it seemed, fell on Reagan's advisers. Central to the complex scam was Oliver North. The marine served as go-between in dealing with the main characters. Testimony revealed that Reagan hadn't played much of a part in the proceedings. His reputation as the Teflon president grew. No problems ever seemed to stick to him.

First Lady

The Reagans successfully fused the worlds of politics and entertainment, of Washington and Hollywood. The Reagans loved celebrities and famous people. Genealogists flattered the Reagans by revealing distant family links to royal houses of Great Britain and Europe. Mrs. Reagan kept signed pictures of Queen Elizabeth II and the Prince and Princess of Wales prominently displayed in her office.

Mrs. Reagan would do almost nothing without consulting her astrologer, Joan Quigley. Nor would she allow her husband to, either. Ms. Quigley had access to the first lady that few others had. The first lady—along with the president's chief of staff—would schedule the president's time according to color-coded days. The system identified days that were safe (green); particularly dangerous (red); or neutral, when anything could happen (yellow).

Mrs. Reagan had always been superstitious, but her obsession seemed to take hold after the assassination attempt on her husband. Ms. Quigley had warned the first family that something harmful might happen on that day. For Nancy, having that dire prophecy fulfilled opened the floodgates.

Nancy Reagan managed the president's schedule, oversaw his staff, recommended dismissals and new appointments, and advised him on political strategies. Not only did Nancy Reagan manage his schedule and staff; she also tried to manage his image. Many people saw her as scheming, wheedling and intimidating.

Nancy Reagan was at her most typical when she met Raisa Gorbachev, the wife of the Soviet leader, during the Gorbachevs' visit to the United States in 1987. A spirit of détente—or gradual improvement of U.S./Soviet relations —had brought the official visit about. Mrs. Reagan probably felt intimidated by this powerful woman from the other side of the world. Mrs. Gorbachev holds a Ph.D. and had studied and taught sociology at the university level.

The press showed the charming Mrs. Gorbachev to have more intellectual substance than Nancy Reagan. Relations between the two women were remarkably cool. Mrs. Gorbachev was in many ways more poised and relaxed. White House sources revealed—and the press picked up on it—that Mrs. Reagan sniffed about Mrs. Gorbachev, "Who does that dame think she is?"

Nancy Reagan wanted to pattern her role as first lady after that of Jackie Kennedy. She wanted to be a first lady of sophistication, high fashion and exquisite taste in interior design. She did make strong statements in all of these areas. She did not succeed in becoming a second Jackie, but she brought her own personal style to the position.

Nancy Reagan finally met Jackie Kennedy at a fund-raiser for the Kennedy library. The women, who had spoken several times on the telephone, could hardly be considered good friends, but they showed a cordial affection for each other.

Nancy Reagan greets children who are participating in the "Just Say NO" campaign.

Mrs. Reagan the Crusader

Early in her career as first lady, Nancy Reagan supported the Foster Grandparents Program. Soon Mrs. Reagan began to notice America's growing drug problem and lent her support to fight drug use in various ways.

Mrs. Reagan is widely credited with spearheading the "Just Say NO" to drugs campaign. In 1985 she became the first first lady in history to address the United Nations. It was a special session devoted to the worldwide problem of drug abuse. The first ladies of some 30 countries were on hand to hear her speech.

It was her idea that the war against drugs had to be fought on a personal, family level—not with costly government programs. Early on, Mrs. Reagan drew criticism for not doing enough to support her cause. Later she appointed advisers to do much of the work.

The First Family

Shortly after President Reagan's inauguration, the Reagan family gathered in the East Room for a group portrait. It was one of the first and last times the whole family got together. They were not particularly close-knit.

Nancy Reagan was a woman who reveled in wielding enormous power. Because of this, she was often aloof from her children. In fact, she would sometimes visit friends and not even speak to her children or grandchildren when she was staying nearby.

The Reagan children were often conspicuously absent from both public functions and private ones. They did not display traditional family values, and the press and public noticed.

Daughter Maureen remained fairly close to her father. A staunch Republican, she did differ with him on certain points. The Equal Rights Amendment was one of these. The act would guarantee greater opportunities for women. Reagan consistently failed to support the measure.

Reagan's son Michael wrote an autobiography disclosing that he had been abused by a camp counselor as a child. This revelation helped bring the important social issue of child abuse out into the open. But it did not bring the Reagans any closer to Michael.

Daughter Patti Davis became permanently alienated from her parents in 1985 when she published a thinly disguised autobiographical novel about a presidential family. Many people recognized her parents in the book's grotesque caricatures.

The Reagans' son Ron pursued a show business career. He became a classical ballet dancer with the Joffrey Ballet. But he was not particularly successful and soon turned to television acting.

Ronald Reagan, Jr., pursued an unsuccessful career as a ballet dancer before turning to acting.

The press has had a field day with the Reagans' dysfunctional family life. The lack of warmth, the bitterness and the resentments within the Reagan family have fueled columnists. The family foibles have been a cause for gloating by political and personal enemies. Many have portrayed Reagan as a bumbling incompetent and Nancy as a social-climbing witch.

The Reagan White House

The Reagans carried out major renovations to the White House private living quarters. Their tastes and decorating needs were very different from the Carters'. They also oversaw large-scale redecoration of the public rooms. They modernized the bathrooms and bought additional art objects for the White House collection.

Nancy Reagan hired Los Angeles decorator Ted Graber to help with her continuing refurbishment of the White House. The Reagans left things in such impeccable condition that President Bush and his wife had almost nothing to do when they moved in after the 1989 inauguration.

There were some 30 rooms in the White House living quarters on the second and third floors. To make their new home cozier, the Reagans brought many pieces of their own furniture from California. Nancy Reagan transformed the third floor billiard room into a room for family memorabilia. Since both Reagans were conscious of fitness, they installed stationary bicycles for workouts. Nancy also had 12 double closets for her personal wardrobe.

Many of Nancy Reagan's stylish clothes were created by well-known designers, and they were given to Nancy for free. By having Nancy show off their clothes, the designers got something free in exchange: good publicity. Nancy did this as late as 1988 despite the fact that in 1982 she had pledged to pay for her clothes. In that year the Internal Revenue Service questioned the fact that Nancy had not declared these gifts as income to be taxed.

The Reagans returned the money due them from Congress for renovations, and privately raised the money to redecorate—eventually an amount totaling $800,000 was spent. Despite the fact that the money had not come from taxpayers, the American public still criticized the Reagans for having spent so much.

Mrs. Reagan's china order was a necessity, as there was no matched set for the State Dining Room, where up to 120 guests might be served at the same time. The china was not purchased with public funds but was a gift from a private foundation. When the china purchase was complete, there were 4,391 pieces, including 220 19-piece place settings and more than 200 serving pieces. The total cost was more than $200,000.

At dinners and lunches—and there were a lot of them—the Reagans almost always served some form of chicken. It was thrifty, nutritious and contained little fat. At one memorable state dinner, the Reagans entertained the Prince and Princess of Wales. The Princess whirled out onto the dance floor with actor John Travolta of *Saturday Night Fever* fame.

In 1981 Nancy Reagan hosted a Christmas party at the White House. The party was for children of the Diplomatic Corps. Mrs. Reagan welcomed some 400 children dressed in their native costumes. Magicians entertained.

Despite the White House elegance, the Reagans missed their California homes. At heart a cowboy, Reagan was nowhere more at home than on the ranch. Nancy preferred a more glamorous lifestyle, but she too enjoyed being away from the limelight.

Act Two

Reagan had little trouble running for reelection in 1984. The economy kept strengthening, and he became immensely popular. The Democrats selected Walter Mondale to run opposite Reagan. And Mondale chose a woman for his vice presidential candidate, Geraldine A. Ferraro of New York.

Ronald and Nancy Reagan dance at the Second Inaugural Ball, in 1985.

39

The Democrats were badly defeated in the election. Reagan won 59 percent of the popular vote, which was one of the highest showings in presidential election history. The only state that Reagan did not carry in the electoral college vote was Mondale's home state of Minnesota.

Reagan was one of the best-traveled American presidents. His trips took him overseas many times. In June 1982 he made a grand tour of four European nations. Both Reagans traveled to China in 1984. And in 1985 they returned to Europe for a meeting with Mikhail Gorbachev in Geneva. In 1986 they went to Tokyo.

In a progressive move aimed at appeasing women's rights advocates, Reagan had selected the first woman Supreme Court justice, Sandra Day O'Connor, in 1981. A staunch conservative, she was easily confirmed by the Senate. She was sworn in at the White House Rose Garden. However, in 1987 Reagan's second nominee for the Supreme Court, Robert Bork, was not as lucky as Ms. O'Connor. Bork did not win the Senate vote necessary to confirm his appointment, so he did not join the court. Perhaps Reagan was beginning to lose his magic touch.

In July 1985 Reagan had a small tumor removed from his colon. Although he recovered quickly, there was little denying that Reagan's most useful years might be coming to an end. As he grew older he suffered an increasing loss of hearing and eventually wore hearing aids in both ears. Nancy also underwent surgery for a cancerous lesion on her lip. Although youthful in appearance and action, the first couple were beginning to show signs of age.

In October 1986 there was a historic meeting in Reykjavik, Iceland, between Reagan and Soviet premier Mikhail Gorbachev. It was a major arms reduction talk, but Reagan seemed to waffle and ramble. It was as if he did not really grasp the proposals that the Soviets were making. He was unprepared and ill equipped for the meeting. Reagan was now 75. Many began to ask if Reagan was too old to be an effective president.

President Ronald Reagan and Soviet premier Mikhail Gorbachev at the summit in Reykjavik, Iceland

After the White House

Reagan left the White House two weeks short of his 78th birthday. Both Reagans have retained vigorous health. Most of their time has been spent on their ranch or at their home in Bel-Air, near Hollywood. The ex-president has continued to ride horses, even after a riding accident required surgery to remove fluid from his brain.

The Reagans retired gracefully, but they have not left the public eye. The publishing firm of Simon & Schuster paid Ronald Reagan $5 million to write his memoirs.

Reagan has commanded as much as $30,000 to $50,000 per speech on the lecture circuit. In 1989 he paid a two-day visit to Japan. The purpose of the visit was to promote better trade relations between the United States and Japan. The publicity junket earned him $2 million. Reagan put the money into the fund for his presidential library.

Reagan remains a respected symbol of the Republican party. One of the few highlights of the lackluster 1992 Republican convention was his appearance and speech.

The Reagan Legacy

Most presidents have left the country a mixed legacy. But Reagan's has been, perhaps, more mixed than most. Probably more than any other president of the 20th century he exemplifies the ideal that just about anyone can grow up to be president.

Reagan was able to parlay his success as governor along with his celebrity status into a successful bid for the presidency. Even before he became president, his name was recognized by nearly every person in America, both from his movie career and his long stint in television.

When Reagan first took office, Americans felt cynical about rising crime, stagnating cities and inflation. Gasoline shortages, the Mideast conflict, hostages and terrorism had all contributed to widespread discouragement.

After the lackluster Carter years, many credit Reagan with revitalizing America's spirit. Domestic and foreign problems did not go away. But Americans began to take a renewed pride in their country. The 1960s and 1970s had seen much of the glitter go out of American life because of Vietnam, Watergate and racial divisions. But the war was long past, and people could once more concentrate on their old values. America could again take its rightful place as the world's number one power.

Reagan was able to turn America's image problem around. But Reagan's critics cite a society that has increasingly turned to greed and self-interest. Industry and government cooperated in weakening the power of labor unions and undermining the rights of America's workers.

It was revealed that the federal Housing and Urban Development agency (HUD) was fraught with mismanagement and misappropriation of funds. Because of loose practices and insider trading scandals, the stock market came to a near collapse in 1987.

The country has also felt the destabilizing influence of the many industries that have been deregulated. The savings and loan (S&L) industry scandal—which cost Americans billions of dollars and unsettled large sectors of the economy—was the creation of professionals uncomfortably close to the top officials in the land. Finally, the Reagan administration gets poor marks for its record on education, the environment and civil rights.

Many blame Reagan for allowing the AIDS epidemic to get out of control. They believe that the government should have stepped in sooner, with warnings, education and additional funding for research into finding a cure for the deadly disease.

Reagan left unfulfilled a conservative political agenda that sought to achieve a federal ban on abortion and the restoration of prayer in the public schools. Two of his goals had more direct implications for the economy. He hoped to pass a constitutional amendment that would require a balanced budget. And he tried to increase the president's power by enacting the "line-item" veto. This would have allowed the president to approve certain parts of a piece of legislation and reject other provisions.

But what President Reagan left in his wake were a severe recession, a weakening dollar and huge government deficits. The nation has witnessed a tremendous growth in poverty, with a burdening of the lower and middle classes. At the same time some people have experienced a newfound prosperity. Economic conditions have created pockets of wealth among the superrich and young urban professionals, or yuppies.

The Reagan legacy has been more mixed than most presidents. It will be some time before we can fully judge Reagan's achievements and failures.

It was probably the right point in American history to have a president who was more than part showman and actor. The country needed some plain talk just to help it find its direction. But the jury is still out on whether our 40th president—the ex-actor—did the country more harm than good.

For Further Reading

Anthony, Carl Sferrazza. *First Ladies: The Saga of the Presidents' Wives and Their Power, Volume II, 1961-1990.* New York: William Morrow and Company, Inc., 1991.

Fisher, Leonard Everett. *The White House.* New York: Holiday House, 1989.

Friedel, Frank. *The Presidents of the United States of America.* Revised edition. Washington, D.C.: The White House Historical Association, 1989.

Friedman, Stanley P. *Ronald Reagan: His Life Story in Pictures.* New York: Dodd, Mead and Company, 1985.

Klapthor, Margaret Brown. *The First Ladies.* Revised edition. Washington, D.C.: The White House Historical Association, 1989.

Lindsay, Rae. *The Presidents' First Ladies.* New York: Franklin Watts, 1989.

The Living White House. Revised edition. Washington, D.C.: The White House Historical Association, 1987.

Menendez, Albert J. *Christmas in the White House.* Philadelphia: The Westminster Press, 1983.

Reagan, Ronald. *An American Life.* New York: Simon & Schuster, 1990.

Robbins, N. *Ronald Reagan: Fortieth President of the United States.* Ada, Oklahoma: Garrett Educational Corporation, 1990.

St. George, Judith. *The White House: Cornerstone of a Nation.* New York: G. P. Putnam's Sons, 1990.

Sandak, Cass R. *The White House.* New York: Franklin Watts, 1980.

Schwartzberg, Renee. *Ronald Reagan.* New York: Chelsea House, 1991.

Sullivan, George. *Ronald Reagan.* New York: Julian Messner, 1985.

The White House. Washington, D.C.: The White House Historical Association, 1987.

Index